# How to Make Money Online

## Easy Ways to Make Extra Cash from Home

Aryla Publishing © 2017

www.arylapublishing.com

*Visit the site for more information on books by* <u>*Fiona Welsh*</u> *and to be informed of* ***free promotions!***

Please see other books in my series

## The Grieving Heart:-

How To Be Strong During A Break Up

How To Deal With Financial Stress

The Great Expectations Of Life

Rock That Body: How To Gain Total Body Confidence

Dealing with Death : Finding Your Way After a Loss

Depression: Dealing With Depression Mental Health
Support

Anxiety: Dealing With Anxiety & Panic Attacks

## Business & Home Series:-

How to Make Money Online

Keeping Your Children Safe

# Contents

# Introduction

Unfortunately, the pot of gold at the end of the rainbow is yet to be found, there doesn't seem to be a Leprechaun smiling at whoever manages to stumble upon this long-famed prize, and as for the money tree, well, it's still as elusive as ever.

From time to time, we all find money hard to come by, and no matter how hard we work, or how much we save, it's likely that there are things we want and need that we can't afford at the present time. Obviously, that doesn't mean that your money situation is going to be difficult all the time, because cash flow ebbs and flows (pardon the pun) as much as anything in life, but finding ways to help it along a little is always a good thing.

The internet has changed so much about our modern-day lives, it is quite hard to think of anything that we don't use an online connection for in some way or another. From booking holidays, doing our grocery shopping, meeting the new Mr or Mrs Right in our lives, or finding a new job, the Internet connects it all. So, taking that thought a little further, can the Internet help us to earn a little extra cash when our flow isn't, well, flowing as fast as we would like?

Of course, it can!

The Internet is a fantastic place to start, and the beauty of all of it is that you can do it from the comfort of your armchair!

This book is for anyone who is wanting to find innovative and enjoyable ways to make a little extra cash, without having to go out and get another job. All you need is an Internet connection, and away you go! Working online is big business for a reason, and there are countless ways you can make a little extra moolah to boost your bank balance.

Now, we do need to highlight one potentially serious issue before we go on to give you the details, and that is about taxes.

It really does depend on your country of origin, but for the most part, you should declare any extra earnings to your Government department related to tax, and pay tax on that income. We can't give you specifics because rules differ from one country to another, so we should just advise you to check out what you need to do in your own particular country.

Serious stuff aside, let's get excited about that extra cash you can be making quicker than you realise!

For many of the ideas and suggestions we're going to discuss, you don't even need to speak to anyone in person, you can simply message via the wonder of the Internet – perfect if you're not feeling quite so sociable!

Working online is ideal for anyone – from stay at home moms and dads, to those who want to work on the side of their regular jobs. Basically, the wonder of technology has changed everything, and made the world a much smaller place. This is fantastic news for your bank balance!

# Ways to Make Cash Online

This book is going to run through a selection of suggestions on how to make extra cash at home, thanks to the Internet's reach. Of course, there may be other ways in addition to the ones we're going to talk about, but the ones we will discuss are tried and tested, and guaranteed to bring a flow of cash towards those who embark upon them.

The suggestions we're going to talk about include:

- Selling on eBay
- Selling on Amazon
- Dropshipping
- Writing eBooks to sell
- Freelancing as a virtual worker, using sites such as Upwork, for instance
- Matched betting
- Investing in penny stocks
- Freelance writing
- Becoming a blogger
- Becoming a Vlogger, on YouTube
- Making things and selling them, on sites such as Etsy and Shopify

In our next chapter, we will go over each one in more detail, and give you advice on how to get into it, what you need to do, how it works, and how much of a success you can expect to make of it. As with anything though, you will get out of it what you put in, and the more hours you can dedicate to the idea, the more extra cash you're likely to make.

## How do You Get Paid?

One of the first questions that many people have is about getting paid. So, how do you get paid? Well, it depends on the option you're going for, and the client you're working with. For instance, if you go through a freelancing site, such as Upwork, you will be paid by the client through the site, which will then be transferred either into your direct bank account, or via a third-party site, such as PayPal. It can be a long process in terms of payments clearing, but it does give you extra protection, and you know that you're going to get paid.

Another way to get paid is directly from the client, either into your bank account or via another site such as PayPal. This does carry a slight amount of risk, simply because there is no guarantee that the client will pay after the job is done? You can minimise said risk, by asking for an upfront payment, or a partial. This is something you need to assess in terms of risk at the time. It may also be the case that you get paid on a certain day per month, such as with book royalties.

Basically, in terms of payments, you need to be very clear when starting the project, to avoid working for nothing.

## Safety & Security

Another area we have to address before we begin involves your safety and security online. This can follow two different routes—ensuring you are working safely online and are not open to virus' or cyber-attacks, but also that you are backing up your work and your equipment as well.

You need two things, aside from everything else:

- Internet security protection (antivirus protection and the like)
- A way to back up your data, e.g. SD card, flash drive, external memory card, or 'cloud' storage

You need antivirus protection whether you are working online or not, because these days we are open to more threats than ever before. There are countless options available to you, and you can either purchase a full protection suite, e.g. McAfee or Norton, or you can download a free version for basic protection, such as AVG. Whichever option you choose, you should always enable updates, and scan your device regularly.

The other thing we mentioned involves backing up your work. This is something you need to do, because if your device is stolen, or something happens and it breaks, you could lose all your work, which could be a minor disaster for your bottom line. You can use an external hard drive or a flash drive pen, some use an SD card, or you could go the more modern route and save your work to the 'cloud' which basically means you don't even need to purchase or carry any other equipment. A few options for that include One Drive or Dropbox.

So, we have covered the important things, and have mentioned tax issues in our introduction, so all that is left to do is get to the nitty gritty of our income earning suggestions, and set you on your way to boosting your cash flow!

# Your Guide to Making Cash Online

Now it's time for the good stuff!

You've obviously picked up this book because you're keen to make some extra cash, and this chapter is going to give you much more practical advice on how to follow each suggestion we have, and help you pick the right one for you.

You should certainly look at your own skills and interests when it comes to finding the right choice for you. It's no good opting for the article writing choice, if you're no good at writing; similarly, it's foolish to go for the idea of selling craft items, if you don't have a crafty bone in your body. Think about what you enjoy doing, and see if you can adapt it to making cash online – you will surely enjoy your new side-line much more as a result, and who knows, it might even turn out to be such a great money maker that you leave your full-time job and dedicate even more time to it!

Let's explore each one in turn.

## Selling Your Junk on eBay

One man's junk is another man's treasure, and in terms of eBay that is a certain truth! If you want to clear your house of rubbish (metaphorically speaking), and you want to earn a little cash at the same time, combining the two is a great way to line your bank account.

Now, this particular option isn't a continuous money spinner, unless you have endless junk that is discovered every week! Having said that, it is possible to turn this into your own online business, with an eBay online store. First however, let's look at selling your own junk.

Decluttering your house is a great suggestion from time to time, because not only does it make room for new things, but it also gives you a much greater sense of order. Having a massive clean out is a great way to give yourself a minor happiness boost (try it, it works!), and when you list the items and sell them on eBay, you could earn a fair bit of cash.

Obviously, for this you're going to need an eBay account, but they are free to sign up for, and you simply link it to your PayPal account, in order to transfer the cash to your bank account at the end. You should know that eBay does take a small cut of your profits, and you generally pay a listing fee on each item, though it's very small. If you start the bid at a higher amount than the basic recommendation, you will see a notice on the screen at the time.

You'd be surprised at what actually sells on eBay, and it's often the things you don't expect to sell which do! Don't outbid yourself by starting your auction too high, but at the same time, don't undercut yourself either. A good idea is to include a Buy It Now price on, which means that if someone wants to literally 'buy it now' they can do so by paying the best price you have stated. If the item doesn't get a 'buy it now' bid, but it does get regular bids, you can decide whether to sell it to the person for that amount, or to try and get your best price bid again. Basically however, if you're selling junk, any cash made is better than nothing!

Another option is to go for an eBay store. This is an online business and you basically sell your items via eBay, listing new items as they become available in your stock. This means you still pay the listing and eBay fees, but it cuts out the need for you to advertise, have your own website and other details, because the eBay platform basically does that hard work for you.

After you have listed the item, you will get a notification from eBay that someone has bought it, then you just have to ship it out and the cash will be transferred to your eBay account. It's quite an easy way to sell goods, but you obviously need to have the goods in the first place in order to dispatch them in a timely manner. The eBay model is all about reputation and ratings, so you need to keep up on your end of the bargain in order to get good customer feedback. This means that people will be much more likely to buy from you in the future.

As you can see, eBay is a good little money spinner, whether you decide to simply sell your junk, or you set up a business. The other perk is that unless you set the postage fee at free, the customer will also pay the cost of shipping, saving you a bit of extra cash.

## Selling Products on Amazon

We won't spend too much time on this particular option, as it is very similar to what we have just mentioned about setting up a business through eBay. Amazon allows you to sell your goods in a very likeminded way, however Amazon is less about second hand goods (although there are some) and more about new products instead.

The same kind of process applies in many ways, you simply sign up for an Amazon seller account and you register your business. This is something you need to do, because unlike eBay, Amazon doesn't let you sell as an individual per se, and you need to be a registered 'store' in their system. This also means that just like eBay, you need to keep your customers happy, by ensuring that you keep your rating as high as possible – five stars is preferable, as most people tend to look toward sellers with a higher rating, to enable them to purchase things with confidence.

Can you make much money with Amazon? Well, you can sell your old items on Amazon too, but this is mainly limited to DVDs, books and technological items as such. In terms of setting up a store, the sky is probably the limit, but you will need to ensure that you have enough stock to meet demand. If you fail to ship your items within the specified time, your rating is going to fall, and you won't get many customers wanting to buy from you.

Just like with eBay, your postage costs are covered, and that means you don't have to worry about finding the extra cash. On the other hand, if you keep your postage costs down, and even free if possible, you are likely to attract more customers, and that means more cash coming your way.

## Dropshipping

The term 'dropshipping' sounds complicated, but the actual theory behind it is not. There is a lot of money to be made with dropshipping, if you can build up your business and keep new products coming in and accessible.

Basically, dropshipping is the process of selling goods to a customer. You have your own business, but you don't have to keep the products in stock. Bear with us!

This means that you acquire the product after you have sold it, which requires that you have a good and reliable relationship with the suppliers that you acquire the products from. There is quite a bit of background work involved with dropshipping, but once you have the supplier relationships established, it can run quite smoothly.

Confused? Let's run a scenario through.

You have set up a dropshipping business specialising in cell phone accessories, e.g. cases, covers, chargers, etc. This is quite a popular one to go for, with a lot of competition, but for the sake of showing you how it works, we'll go down this route.

Before you start anything, you will contact suppliers and find out what products they have available, and you will start a working relationship with them. You will go to them when you have sold something to a customer. You will advertise the products that you can freely find, and you don't have to work with just one supplier. You can use several, and you will sell them to customers online. Once a customer buys a product, you will contact the supplier and order it. The supplier will then dispatch the product and you don't have to worry about posting anything out.

The money is shared between you and the supplier, as you obviously have to pay the supplier for the product, keeping a share for yourself. Your price has to reflect this, otherwise you're not going to make any money!

Dropshipping is an ever growing home business phenomenon, and it is something you can easily do online, without an office, or any other start-up equipment, other than a laptop, Internet connection, and perhaps a telephone in case of any issues with suppliers. You can easily branch out into as many different areas of specialism as you like, provided you have the reliable suppliers to work with.

The downside? The ability to find reliable suppliers in the first place. If you pick the wrong ones, you're going to end up with very disgruntled customers, and this is not going to turn into an easy way to make cash online. New starters in the dropshipping world may also find it difficult to search out some of the more top quality suppliers, because you just don't have any history in the business. This can be overcome with a firm business plan however, and while this might sound like a complicated way to make a bit of extra cash, it needn't be that way, provided you have a clear strategy in terms of what you want to achieve.

Put simply, while dropshipping is a good way to make a little extra cash on the side, it is also a very real possibility that it could grow into something much larger, and before time, you could have a real business of your own which makes you more than just a little 'extra' money!

## Writing eBooks to Sell

A newer phenomenon these days is eBooks. How many times do you go into a book store and buy an actual paperback or hardback version of a book now? Probably not that much. Whilst we all still love to hold a fresh, shiny new book, it's just not what is done in our modern times, and instead, we grab our smartphone or tablet, scan for what we want and read it there. You can basically download a book on any subject you want these days, and that fact opens up the world of writing your own eBooks, or getting someone else to do it, and then selling them to make royalty cash.

Now, if you're a keen writer, this is a great way to get your name published, and even though you are doing it in a self-publishing manner, e.g. you're not contacting an outside supplier, that doesn't matter! Your name is on a book, and for many that is enough.

On the other hand, if you're not someone who can write eBooks, or even write at all, you can still use this avenue to make cash, by hiring someone to do the writing process for you. Head online to freelancing sites and hire a writer to do the creative bit, ask them to sign a ghost-writing agreement, which basically hands over all the rights to you, pay them their fee, and then the book is yours to sell. This is a very common method these days, and one which can be very lucrative, if the standard of the book is up to scratch.

Of course, you need to find a freelance writer who has a high standard of writing, because selling eBooks is all about reviews. You will find that if you rack up several poor reviews, your book is not going to show up in searches very well, and you're not going to make money. For that reason, look for freelancers with good testimonials on their work, set out your expectations before the work begins, and then ask for a mid-way check in, just to see how the book is shaping up.

It's also a good idea to head online, to sites like Amazon, to find out what kinds of subjects are trending at the moment. It's no good writing a book on an obscure subject that nobody is going to want to read about, because similarly, nobody is going to buy it! On the other hand, if you can identify the subjects that are in vogue at the moment, you can ride the wave of fashion, and grab some readers.

When self-publishing books on Amazon, the process is not particularly hard. You simply upload the book to the site, e.g. Amazon Kindle, CreateSpace, and from there you will be guided through the process. The book will be checked by Amazon for any plagiarism, so this is something you need to be mindful of, running it through Copyscape first to check for any duplications. Before the book is checked by Amazon, you will create the format, e.g. the cover, the pages, how you want it to look, etc. This can be time consuming, because you want the front cover to be attractive, and to grab a readers' attention. Then, you simply submit the book for final checking, and you wait around five days for your answer.

From there, your book will show on the Amazon site, and people can purchase it. You will be paid a royalty fee every time someone buys a book, with Amazon taking a small amount of it as well. Of course, in order to make more money, you need to market the book, and this is something you'll need to consider also. Share it on social media, get friends to leave you a good review, and the more stars you get, the higher up the rankings your book will show.

Your royalties will be paid into your dedicated bank account every month, and you can also have several books on the go, you don't have to just stick to one. Once the initial process is done, and the book it out there, getting reviews and gathering interest, you basically sit there and wait for the cash to hit your account!

## Freelancing as a Virtual Worker

This is a method I can vouch for! If you have a skill, e.g. organisational or creative, then there are many ways you can use that skill to make a little extra cash on the side. The main plus point of this is also that you get to pick your hours, and work it around your regular daily tasks. Of course, the more work you do, the more money you get, but if you just want something for a little extra income, pick and choose your projects wisely, to compliment your lifestyle.

Head online and check out the best freelancing websites to join, but do be aware that you should never be asked for money when signing up to a website. This is a red flag to look out for, because the best freelancing sites, e.g. Upwork and Freelancer, for example, are free to join, and will never ask you for cash. Upwork does have an upgrade you can purchase, with additional perks not available in the regular free membership basic package, but this is a personal decision to make, and many people find that the basic option is more than enough for them at the beginning.

Once you've signed up and created a profile, you're free to look for jobs to apply for. Again, freelancing is all about reputation and rankings, so if you're going to take on a job, make sure you can complete it in a timely manner and to a high standard to avoid bad reviews, which will impact your ability to get future work.

Clients will then post the jobs that they want to be done, and it's up to you to decide which ones to go for. You can search for criteria that suits your needs, such as blogging, transcription, virtual assistant, creative design, etc., and then place a bid or application for the job.

If successful, you will be hired, a contract will be set up virtually, and you are free to do the job, then submit the final piece. Upon approval, your payment will be cleared and sent to your account, which can then be transferred to your bank account via a variety of different ways, e.g. direct deposit, PayPal, Payoneer, wire transfer, etc. You can choose your preference in terms of payment, from the options available on the site you are working with.

Virtual assistants are some of the most popular jobs to be listed on these sites. This type of job is almost like a PA or assistant/secretary, but instead of going into work every day, you sit at home on your laptop, or wherever you are in the world, and you answer emails, post on social media, eBay, etc., create travel plans, and stay in touch with your client via Skype or email. This is the modern day way of having a personal assistant, and provided you can work within the same time zone (roughly), and you can commit to a set number of hours, working flexibly, this is a great money spinner.

Many virtual assistant jobs are paid by the hour, so make sure that you set a fair hourly rate. This money will then be logged by the freelancing site every week, and then you will receive it into your account around 10 days later, varying from site to site. You can choose to manually log your time, or you can use an app to track how much time you're working – this will depend on the preference of the client, and is something you can talk about at the time of hiring, or as you gain trust between the two of you.

Again, virtual work as a freelancer is something you can build up over time to become a full-time job, or you can use it to simply earn cash on the site, the choice is yours.

## Matched Betting

The world of online betting can be a confusing one if you have no idea about odds and how it all works, but if you are someone who does bet occasionally, or you're someone who is happy to learn about it, then matched betting could be a way for you to earn some extra cash, all from the comfort of your armchair at home, with an Internet connection as your only friend!

Matched betting is about taking advantage of offers from large betting companies, such as Betway or Bet365, to name just a few. For instance, you would find a company which had an offer on, e.g. you deposit around $30 to start up, and you bet it on a sport or event which has odds which are around the even mark. The offer should then be that when the bet is placed, you'll get an extra $30 for a free bet. This is to entice you into betting more – do be aware that online betting can be very addictive, and you'll need to remain grounded, so as not to let the beast out, and you become far more into it than you should be!

Having said that, if you can keep your eyes firmly on just making a little extra cash, rather than betting everything you own, matched betting could be a good option for you.

Back to our example – with your new $30 free bet, you place it wisely, and the hope is that you will win some cash. Whether you withdraw that and keep it, or you re-bet it, that's your choice, but in order to make money from this, you need to keep re-betting your winnings, in the hope that you will get a snowball effect.

Does it work? Well, many people use it, so it definitely has some kudos!

Shop around for the best offers, because some signup initiatives can be really rewarding, and you want to get the best first deposit deal that you can – this gives you more chances of winning, because you have more cash to bet with from the get-go.

A word of warning, we have mentioned this already, but we need to go over it one more time. If you are going to go into matched betting as a way of making extra cash at home, only bet with your free bet winnings, and never add a little extra to top up the pot. If you do this, you may begin to start on a slippery slope, and you'll be betting cash you don't have, losing money, rather than making it. This is something you need to avoid at all costs! Of course, this doesn't happen to everyone, far from it, but it is a very real risk that you need to know about and address. If you can keep yourself on an even keel, and avoid this happening, then by all means, go for it!

Matched betting is a great way to earn cash, and get a little excitement, especially for those who enjoy sporting events, or even events in real life. These days we can bet on anything, from the winner of the latest TV talent show to the sex of the new royal baby! It doesn't have to be about soccer and horse racing, although these will probably always be the most popular types of betting routes.

## Investing in Stocks & Shares (Penny Stocks)

Do you know a little about investments? If so, penny stocks could be a great way for you to break into the stocks and shares market, and potentially earn yourself some extra cash online.

Online you will see all manner of investment opportunities, some as low as $1. Now, you'd look at that investment and think that it's just not going to make you anything, right? Well, with a little patience, you may find that the value of that $1 soon jumps up to $100, and then possibly even $1000. It's a game of chance, and it is a game that can be done online, with quite a lot of big winners.

When trying to find the best penny stocks to buy, look at the following factors:

- **Does the company you're investing in actually make cash?** – It's no good investing in a company that is going under, so always do a little research into the company itself, and make sure that it is a money spinner, either now or predicted to be in the future.

- **Does the company have a lot of assets?** – If the company gets into trouble, they need a large amount of assets to survive the problem. A lot of companies get into strife every now and then, but you need to pick a company that is able to get through that time, and survive through to the other side, prospering onwards.

- **Is the company listed on the stock exchange?** – Many penny stock opportunities aren't listed, but if you find one that is, then that company is worth an investment, for sure. You can easily find this information out online.

Out of all the methods of making money online that we've talked about, investing in penny stocks is probably the most difficult to explain in terms of success. This is because it is all a game of chance, and nobody can really give you a definite 'yes' in terms of whether you're going to make money. On the other hand, the chances that you will make cash are still there, and many people have made a good income from penny stocks in the past. Obviously, bigger cash investments are always much safer, but if you're just investing $1, surely, it's worth a go, right?

The key here is to buy your stock cheaply, and then watch it. When it starts to make money, sell it. Then you can reinvest. Why? Because if you wait too long, the chances are you might lose cash in the end; yes, it's double edged sword in many ways, because you could equally see that the company's profits go into the stratosphere! That's the nature of the best unfortunately. This is also the option which is likely to take the longest time to bring you any cash flow, but if you're not in a rush, a few penny stocks could bring you an influx over a little time.

## Freelance Writing

Do you have a 'thing' for words? Are you able to research a subject and then create content based on what you have learnt? Are you able to write stories that come from somewhere in your mind? If so, freelance writing could be a great little money earner on the side for you. In addition, if you manage to build up a good reputation and keep your business going, you could turn this into another full-time job – many people dream of being a writer, and if you have the skills, it's actually easier than you might think.

Again, this is down to those freelancing sites we mentioned earlier, with Upwork being the most popular. When you create your profile, you will need to specify that you are a freelance writer first and foremost, and whilst you can branch out into other wordy areas, such as proofreading or transcription, make sure that writing is your number one concern, in order to attract the right kind of clients.

You will see thousands of writing jobs listed every single day on Upwork, but you also need to know that competition for these jobs is fierce with a capital F! Having said that, not every writer that applies is going to get the job, and not every writer that applies is actually any good at writing! For that reason, you need to make your application bullet proof, and you need to write a couple of sample pieces that you can submit with your application. Start with the smaller jobs, get some five star feedback, and then work up to the bigger jobs; having said that, if you really feel like you can do one of the bigger jobs, but you're a newbie on the site, just apply anyway, you never know!

You could be asked to write an article on absolutely anything; it could be a blog post, it could be an eBook, it could be a technical piece of writing, or it could be an informational article – this is where you get to choose. If you don't like writing technical content, simply don't apply for that type of job; don't be dragged into the idea of thinking that you need to apply for everything to get a good freelancing reputation – if you can't do the job, you're going to get bad feedback, and in this game, feedback is everything.

Stick to the subjects you enjoy; for instance, if you love to travel and see new places, look into travel writing, because that way you will enjoy what you're writing about and the process will not seem like a job, it will be much more of a pleasure to do, whilst earning money at the same time!

You don't have to stick to Upwork when looking for freelance writing gigs, but it is by far the safest way in terms of getting paid. There are many online forums and groups where you will find jobs, including many Facebook groups, but when you agree to work with someone, do be aware that there is no guarantee you're going to get paid. For this reason, it's a good idea to ask for a contract to be drawn up, or to ask for a 50% upfront fee. This means you have more peace of mind that your cash is going to be real at the end of the hard work, and they're not simply going to take your creative musings and run, without giving you what you deserve.

Do not expect to make a fortune from freelance writing, especially at the very start, but this is something that can be built up over time, and can still be a good money spinner on the side.

## Becoming a Blogger

Blogging is big business these days. Once upon a time you used to start a blog just to write about whatever was going on in your life, show it to the outside world, and get nothing for it other than personal satisfaction, but now blogging is a genuine way to make money. It takes hard work to build up your blog and get followers and views, and you will need to hustle to get contacts for advertising revenue, but once that is in place, blogging can be an enjoyable and lucrative way to earn cash on the side.

So, what do you want to blog about? Do you want to blog about the place you live, e.g. make it into a travel guide for that destination, do you want it to be a diary-type of blog, perhaps following the life you lead on your travels again, or just in the work line that you're currently in? Are you a parent and you want to document the trials and tribulations of parenthood? Basically, it needs to be something you enjoy, something you can find creative fun in, and it also needs to be something which is going to resonate with readers. The aim here is to grab attention, keep it, and then keep attracting more. And much like Facebook likes and Instagram likes, the more followers the better!

Setting up a blog is easy, and there are countless sites out there which can help you create a good, free layout, such as WordPress or Wix. Of course, if you want a really professional-looking site then you will have to pay, but there are also packages available through these types of site which give you an annual fee or a monthly fee, and for that you get your own personal domain name, plus more in the way of layout scope and creativity. If you want to really push your blog forward, then it's definitely worth thinking about paying for a more upmarket type of site, rather than the free version; this is fine for hobby-type blogs, and even just to begin, but over time you will want to give yourself a bit of an upgrade.

Once you've identified your subject matter and created your website, you'll need to push it forward, to get readers. There are countless blogs, literally millions, which exist on the Internet, and which are barely even read. This is because the blogger doesn't put any effort into marketing it, using Google SEO tools (Search Engine Optimisation), and doesn't pay much attention to really making it fly. You need to be on the ball, and you need to know what your readers want; you need to use Google Analytics Tools, and this is something you will need to learn about, in order to use them to their maximum potential. If you can get your head around it, and it's really not that hard once you get going, make use of the top keywords to attract attention and to make sure that your blog is high up on Google's search results, then you will find that readers will slowly but surely flock to your page. It takes time with blogging, the results aren't instant, but they are very enjoyable and addictive once you see those numbers creeping up!

In terms of making cash from blogging, you need to think about the following areas:

- **Using advertisements on your site** – You will be paid a small amount every time one of your readers clicks on the advert.
- **Market goods and services for companies and organisations you have a reciprocal agreement with** – This works on a commission basis, and you'll get cash every time someone makes a purchase, having been directed from your site.
- **Sell products for someone else** – You can team up with someone who is selling a product, e.g. someone else who is working online to make extra cash, perhaps selling craft items, and sell them together via your blog. This arrangement works to the advantage of both, and you will split the revenue.
- **Sell services** – This is a similar type of thing, and you will be paid a commission when someone purchases a service from the third-party person you're working with.

You will find that many bloggers create online content, e.g. a blog post, which includes a keyword, and that keyword is a link to a third-party site. For instance, if you're working with a car hire company in Madrid, you'll want to write a blog post about the great things to see and do in Madrid, and within that blog, you'll seamlessly (so nobody even realises you're selling something), mention something about car hire, inserting a hyperlink in the most suitable place. The hope is that the person reading it will be so enthralled by your blog post that they will want to immediately go to Madrid and hire a car, clicking on the link. You'll earn commission from that click if they actually go through with the hire. This is a very common way to make cash on blogs.

The chances are that the more readers you have, the more companies will be willing to work with you in the first place, so you need to focus on pushing up your readership as a first port of call.

## Becoming a Vlogger on YouTube

Do you love to talk, do you love the camera? If so, vlogging could be your route to cash! Vlogging is basically blogging, but without the written words, and using your speech instead. This is ideal for anyone who doesn't really have a passion for writing, and someone who is much better in terms of actually speaking. Writing isn't for everyone, just like speaking isn't for everyone!

The way to make money with vlogging is very similar to blogging, because it's all about advertising products. You will then get a cut of commission whenever one of your viewers makes a purchase, when directed from your site.

You'll find beauty vlogging is big business these days, and that is because there are so many products out there that people want honest opinions on before they buy them. You can then create a tutorial type of video, e.g. how to use primer, and you can showcase the product you're trying to sell. Many businesses will be happy to send you a tester for your troubles, and if not, you'll simply buy it yourself and reap back the cost.

Of course, this type of money making scheme is not only about beauty products, because you can try and recommend any type of product or service you like. For instance, if you've recently been to Italy on a sightseeing tour, you could combine your efforts with an excursion office you used, and you could talk about how you went to the Colosseum, talking about how wonderful it was, and then mention the tour office you booked it through. This could then generate them business, and you get a cut of it. See how easy it can be?

Another way is to have an advert within your video. So, if you don't particularly want to try and sell a product or service yourself, and you simply want to talk about something on your vlog that you do in your general life, you could have an advert placed at the bottom of the video, which will be visible to your viewers whilst you're talking. This means if they click on it and make a sale, you get a cut of the action.

Easy!

The problem with vlogging is that not everyone wants to be on camera or has the inherent charisma to make it truly successful.

## Make & Sell

If you love to make things, such as clothing, jewellery, accessories, home items, basically anything, then you can use that passion to make cash. When you think about it, you're actually doing something you love for money, and that is the real aim in life!

Of course, you can sell these locally, perhaps at craft fairs and local markets, or you could go online and branch out a little, potentially reaching many more people as a result. You can use Facebook, setting up a business page and selling your items that way, or you could use other sites such as Etsy or Shopify. Setting up your own online store means that you can create bespoke items and reach the people who are interested in what you make.

Of course, you're going to need to cover your costs, so make sure that whatever it costs to make the item, plus a little profit, plus postage fees is covered in the amount you sell your item for – but don't go over the top! Again, you're looking at getting repeat customers and/or word of mouth sales, so make sure that you don't slack on customer service.

Shopify certainly looks professional and is a very popular way to reach people; you could also add in a blog or Facebook page to work alongside your Shopify or Etsy page, which would work to bring you more profit.

What you sell is really up to you, and you definitely need to think about what you enjoy, in order to make this a labour of love, rather than just a labour overall. Bespoke clothing is a very popular option at the moment, as well as jewellery and accessories, but people sell everything they have made on these sites, including home furnishings, furniture, pictures, artwork, basically anything! The sky is the limit with this one.

## A Few Low Income Ideas ...

Of course, it may be that you just don't have a lot of time to throw at your extra money making endeavours, but you just want something potentially quick and easy. That is perfectly fine and there are a few ways you can earn a little cash, without putting in extra time. These items aren't likely to bring you huge monetary rewards, but they will bring you some, and that could be just enough for you.

Let's check out three of the easiest ways to give your bank balance a little online boost from time to time.

## Selling Your Photographs Online

Are you a keen photographer? Do you go out at the weekends walking and snap away happily on your phone? If so, are there some fantastic photos on there that you think could be sellable? If so, check out stock photography websites and see if they are currently purchasing photos from users. Sites like Flickr are great for photo sharing and making a little cash, if you want to go down the route of copyright protection.

Do bear in mind that once you sell your photos, you are giving up ownership rights, so you can't use them again for your own credit. If you don't really mind about this however, selling your photos is a great way to enjoy your photography hobby, whilst earning a little extra cash at the same time.

## Online Surveys and Questionnaires

This isn't going to bring you massive gains instantly, but over time, if you want to put in five minutes here and there, there are some cash flow incentives to be had. If you're bored of an evening, or perhaps on a long journey and you have an Internet connection, register with a survey site which pays for your opinion. You can simply click a few boxes and earn cash as you go. The money will mount up the more surveys and questionnaires you do, and is usually deposited into your account every month, or when you reach a certain amount of cash earned.

If you love to give your opinion, this is a great way to earn cash!

## Sell Your Story Online

Do you have a juicy story to tell? Do you want to get your side of things out there? If so, write it all down and submit it to a magazine via email. This means you can usually get paid a set amount for your story, if they choose to print it, and who knows, you might get famous!

There are also magazines who pay for fiction stories to be sent in every month, so you could have a go at that too if you love to write short stories in your spare time.

Creativity is a money maker!

## Do Any of These Ideas Grab Your Attention?

We have talked about a lot of online money making options throughout this long chapter, and all of them are great in their own right. The most important thing when choosing an option however is to make sure that you are going down the route of something you're going to enjoy. This is not work, this is not something you HAVE to do, it is something you want to do, and which brings monetary rewards at the end of it all.

Think about your personality, your likes, your dislikes, and how much time and effort you realistically can put into it. If you are short on time, be honest about this, and instead, look towards one of the options which doesn't require a lot of time or attention, such as matched betting or penny stocks, for instance. If, however you want to be a bit more hands on, then blogging or freelancing is a great money earner, and potentially something which has the power to work up to being a full-time job in the future. These things start off as small acorns, but they have the power and potential to really grow into great things, perhaps even huge trees!

# Hints & Tips for Working Online

We mentioned a little at the start of this book about the things you need to pay attention to when you are working online, but for ease of reference, and to pull it all together, let's recap it all one more time.

When you are working online, you are still working, and that means you need to tick a few boxes.

## Balance

Work, home, and social life balance is key if you want to have a harmonious life. It's very easy to become so excited and enthralled about the idea of making cash, that you allow it to take over, but this is not a good thing, especially if you already have a full-time job.

For instance, if you are working as a freelancer in your spare time, e.g. evenings and weekends, and you are work the rest of the time, do not allow your freelancing hours to become muddled into your actual working hours. Your employer will certainly not be too happy about it, and there could be a real clash of interests. The worst case scenario could be that you lose your full-time job, because your employer feels that you aren't dedicating your time to the cause. This is not something you want, and it is certainly not something that will be positive for your bank account!

On the other side of the coin, you need to be aware that online working for a little extra money is supposed to be fun. We talked about choosing something you enjoy, and this is a definite do. You spend your days doing a job that perhaps you don't enjoy, and that means that when you go home, you don't want to find yourself doing something that you aren't enjoying again! Balance it up and make sure that the online work you are doing gives you a happy boost, and doesn't become a chore.

## Red Tape

We talked earlier about tax issues, and this is so vitally important that we need to cover it again here. If you are working online, you are effectively self-employed, and that means that you need to pay tax on those earnings. How you do this will vary from country to country, so to get the best and most up to date information for you as an individual, you need to venture online and find out from your government's website.

For the most part however, you will pay a percentage of tax on what you earn, and you will usually do this by declaring how much you have earnt in your self-employed work, at the end of the tax year. There are sometimes things you can offset against this, like if you are working full time in another job, if you have assets, etc., but again, this is something you need to look into.

It is a good idea to know what the self-employment percentage of tax is in your country, because then you can simply save it out of your earnings every time you are paid. This money can then be put into a high interest savings account, and when tax payment time comes, the cash is already there, and you don't have to worry about finding a large lump sum of money. The idea is that earning extra money is a good thing, a benefit, and not a hindrance that actually leaves you out of pocket! By putting this money into a high interest savings account, you can also be earning on the interest rate too. Double bonus!

## Internet Security

This is another subject we touched upon, but it is another very vital part of online working. Always make sure that you download a high quality Internet security program for your device, be it a laptop, desktop computer, smartphone, tablet, or anything else. These days we are more at risk of cyber-attacks than ever before, and unless you want to risk losing everything, including your device, then you should make sure you find a good quality program.

This should include anti-virus software, malware and spyware protection, as well as being updated regularly as new initiatives come onto the market. You can download free protection, which will give you the basic amount of protection you need, or you can purchase a suite, which is going to cost more but will probably give you more in the way of overall protection. This is a personal choice and something you need to weigh up for yourself. Either way, make sure you have something in place – anything is better than nothing!

Having a regular back up process is also something you need to consider. This could be working with virtual cloud storage, so you can access your files anywhere in the world with an Internet connection, or it could be having an external hard-drive, but always remember that devices are prone to malfunctions from time to time, and if this is a serious one, you could be losing much more than your hardware, especially if you have been working hard on a long document.

## The Benefits of Working Online Overall

Yes, this book is about making extra money online, but we also need to consider potential growth in the future. What if you enjoy your online money making so much that you want to leave your current job and make it a full-time deal? It can be done, but you need to do some careful planning first.

Let's check this idea out.

The main benefits of online working overall are:

- You can work from anywhere in the world.

- All you need is a device (laptop, tablet, smartphone) and a good quality Internet connection.
- You can use virtual cloud storage, so you don't need to have a lot of expensive hardware.
- The opportunities available are growing year upon year, as this becomes a really popular way to work.
- You can work your own hours, depending on the needs of your lifestyle.

Of course, everything in life has a downside, and to give you a really thorough overview of this type of vocation, we need to cover the disadvantages, too.

- You need to be very motivated and organised. This is because when you go to a normal job, you get up and go to an office, and you don't really have a choice. But when you are working online, you can be distracted by all manner of things, and if you don't do the work, you simply don't get paid!
- Money is not guaranteed. You're not going to have the safety net of a set salary going into your bank every month, as with every type of self-employed work. This uncertainty could be an issue for some.

As you can see, there are more advantages than disadvantages, so once you get your online income earning plan running, see if this is something you would like to branch into in the future, in a more set employment kind of way.

# Conclusion

And there we have it! We are at the end of our book about how to make extra cash online, and by now you should be feeling inspired, excited, and raring to go!

All of the ideas we have covered are accessible to all, and you need to really think about which one suits your personality and skill set the most. As we have mentioned a few times, make sure you pick something which you are going to enjoy – this is meant to be fun, as well as profitable!

Remember to run over the red tape issues, and all the other hints and tips, to make sure that you are covering all bases when it comes to taxes and security, but other than that, making a bit of extra money on the Internet is a fantastic way to boost your bank balance.

You don't have to make this into a future career move, but the scope is certainly there if you want to consider it at some point in the future – think about it as you work, and see if you could branch out and really enjoy your job, on a full-time basis.

*Thank you for reading my book.*

*I would love it if you could leave me an honest review on what you thought of this book.*

*If you like to know more about my books and the opportunity to be notified of free promotions please visit www.ArylaPublishing.com*

*Or follow Facebook Twitter or Instagram*

*Thank you*

# Other Publications

**<u>How to be a World Leader</u>** – By Tyler Moses (Comedy)

The year is 2017 and while none of us know what the future will hold at present we are at the mercy of a world leader in the USA that did not seem possible. But it has happened some ask how? Some ask why? But there is support out there so I say if he can do it then so can I and so can you!

If you are not automatically born into it and lucky enough to be an heir to a kingdom (we will also cover how to bump yourself up the ranks) if you have the unfortunate sibling line to contend with that does not put you in prime position.

In the world, we live in today with technology at our fingertips we have more control and access to information so make use of it the world is your oyster if you have visions of being the most powerful person in the world and have an unstoppable ego then this could be the job for you.

## How to be strong during a Break Up – By Fiona Welsh (Self Help)

When it happens, well, it can feel like the depths of hell, quite frankly; there are tears, recriminations, questions, upset, 'what if', blame, worry about the future, and a million other thoughts and emotions, but the bottom line is that it hurts – a break up *hurts*.

You probably won't want to jump straight back into normal life, even if you try and tell yourself that 'life goes on', and it's not a good idea to do that anyway; you need to go through the grieving stages of a break up, just as you would if you lost someone you loved dearly for other reasons. Don't be surprised if you feel bad, and don't be concerned by this, you need to go through this in order to come out of it the other side.

This book is written from a personal perspective, from personal experience, and this fact means you can trust what you are reading. I myself have suffered that epic break up, and at the time I thought my life was finished; obviously it wasn't, because I'm writing this book, and I want to help you recover from your heartache too, step by step. I have actually been on both sides of the coin, I have been the breaker-upper, and the one who was broken up with; I'm not sure which was worse to be honest, but the good news is that I'm still standing, and so will you.

## Keeping Your Children Safe – By Fiona Welsh
## (Self Help – Business)

Without a doubt, the most important and treasured things we have in our lives are our children. We give birth to them, we raise them, we worry about them, and we love them to the end of the world and back again. It is no surprise that when we see worrying events on the news, it first makes us think of our children.

We can't protect our kids from everything in life, and we can't shield them from the things that are going on around the globe, but we can do our very best to keep them as safe as possible. As a parent you will no doubt be very familiar with the thought that you want to wrap your children up in cotton wool and avert their eyes from anything that isn't Disney magical. Things can and do happen, but part of the solution is to know how to teach your children about safety in general, in the right way. Learning to show them that it is fine to explore, fine to live, but that being on the lookout for danger is vital.

So, how do you do that? How do you tread that fine line between living life and avoiding dangerous situations?

**Sisters Book 1** – By Paula Parsons (Drama)

Your day will come. The light will eventually shine through the cracks of life. You will succeed. You will be happy. ...

Happiness...feeling whole, feeling purposeful...such a beautiful, uplifting thought.

Unfortunately, this is not my story...not even close. I wish I could tell you lies, and say that I come out in the end of all of this, feeling empowered, free, satisfied; happy...

But I don't. Not by a long shot.

My name is Melanie Loomis. I am twenty-seven years old. This is my story.........

Coming Soon

## Julia's Dilemma – By Lyndsey Carter (Romantic Comedy)

Julia sighed as she stepped onto the escalator. As it moved and took her up, she sighed again. Another boring day and another crammed ride home on a smelly train with no seats. She longed for some excitement, something to shake things up. She was sick of the same old, same old.

Julie boarded the train, already knowing as she craned her neck to scan each corner that there would not be any seats open. Instead, she settled for a hand-hold on the pole near the back wall. But her surroundings ceased to bother her as she stared off into the distance and let her thoughts roam. She looked at the houses she passed and imagined what type of people lived there. The train line ran at the back of the houses giving Julie a view of the garden. Some gardens had washing hanging up; others had kids' toys. Some gardens were overgrown like a mini jungle. It was a little daydream game Julie liked to play when she didn't have a book or paper to read. Soon the passing gardens and motion of the train made her eyes heavy.

Julia fought to keep her eyes open, scared that she would miss her stop. Even after six years of riding the same train back and forth to work, she was still afraid that she would fall asleep and ride until the train reached the end of the line.

The mechanical voice announced the train's next stop, and that was enough to wake Julia. She elbowed her way to the front door and stood with the other people who always got off at this stop. Julia didn't smile at them or really register their presence. They all mutually existed without communicating.

**The Truth About Getting Old** – By Tyler Moses
(Comedy)

Congratulations and welcome to the over 40s
club! You have worked hard to get to this pinnacle
point in life, so let's take a moment to celebrate
being over 40 and everything that comes with it.
Your body has been through a lot in order to get
you over the hill, and your 40s is when some of
your parts may start to, well, retire. During your
time in the old person club, your body will
experience new and not-so-exciting changes
around every corner (even though we take
corners slowly now as to avoid obstacles that may
knock us off balance). Grab your Biotene and a
large supply of antacids and sit back on your
heating pad as we journey into the life of being
over 40.

We also have a selection of Adult Coloring Books to help relax pass the time and de-stress.

Beautiful Illustrations and puzzles in the back for your entertainment

Visit Aryla Publishing website to sign up for new release books and free promotions

www.ingramcontent.com/pod-product-compliance
Lightning Source LLC
Chambersburg PA
CBHW071423200326
41520CB00014B/3550